100
Bible Quiz
Activities
for Church
School
Classes

100 Bible Quiz Activities for Church School Classes

James H. & R. Darline Robinson

CONCORDIA

Publishing House
St. Louis

Concordia Publishing House, St. Louis, Missouri
Copyright © 1981, Concordia Publishing House

Printed in the United States of America

1   2   3   4   .5   6   7   8   9   10   CPC   90   89   88   87   86   85   84   83   82   81

Library of Congress Cataloging in Publication Data

Robinson, James H   1930-
      100 Bible quiz activities for church school classes.

      1. Bible games and puzzles. I. Robinson, Rowena D., joint author.
II. Title.
GV1507.B5R6   207   80-24961
ISBN 0-570-03829-4

To the children and teachers of
Peace Lutheran Church
Arvada, Colorado

Foreword

The busiest church school day has a leftover corner of time or could use a change of pace. To fill that time gap profitably and enjoyably, here are 100 Bible activities for middle and upper grade Sunday, weekday, vacation Bible school, and Christian day school teachers and classes that require little or no preparation and few or no materials.

Children will love the challenge and variety of activities as they learn and review Bible information. These Bible quiz activities can be used singly or in clusters, depending on the amount of time available.

A usage chart may be found at the end of the book for teachers to note the date and class when a quiz was used.

—The Authors

1. Location of Bible Cities

Objective: To know the location of Bible cities.

Materials Needed: None.

The Activity: Prepare a list of Bible cities according to your class's knowledge. Children will tell if the city is located in *Galilee, Samaria, Judea,* or *Beyond Palestine. Examples:*

1. Bethlehem—Judea
2. Jerusalem—Judea
3. Capernaum—Galilee
4. Shechem—Samaria
5. Tyre—Beyond Palestine
6. Lystra—Beyond Palestine
7. Bethany—Judea
8. Nazareth—Galilee

2. What Is It?

Objective: To identify Bible geographical names.

Materials Needed: None.

The Activity: Prepare a list of Bible geographical names. As you give a name to the children, ask them to answer with its description—city, country, river, lake, or mountain. Divide the class into groups if you wish. *Examples:*

Cities	Mountains	Lakes or Seas	Rivers	Countries
Jerusalem	Hermon	Gennesaret	Jordan	Macedonia
Nain	Sinai	Tiberius	Tigris	Greece
Bethany	Nebo	Mediterranean	Arnon	Syria
Rimmon	Ebal	Merom	Jabbok	Babylonia
Beersheba	Olives		Euphrates	Galatia
Hebron	Pisgah			Palestine

3. What Picture Would You Take?

Objective: To think of people and places associated with Bible locations.

Materials Needed: None.

The Activity: Suggest to the children to imagine a visit to one of the Bible cities mentioned in the Old or New Testament. Ask them to recall what object or person is mentioned as being in that city, and then to tell what picture they would take if they were a photographer on assignment. *Examples:*

> Nazareth—Joseph's and Jesus' carpenter shop
> Jerusalem—the temple
> Shechem—Jacob's Well
> Bethany—Mary and Martha's home
> Damascus—Straight Street
> Zoar—destruction of Sodom and Gomorrah
> Capernaum—Sea of Galilee

4. Who Made the Headlines?

Objective: To recall which people were associated with a Biblical event.

Materials Needed: Chalkboard.

The Activity: Suggest an event of the Bible and ask children to name the people who would have made the headlines, if the account were written in modern newspaper form. *Examples:* Write these headlines on the board:

Holy Week	*Destruction of Sodom & Gomorrah*	*Plagues of Egypt*	*Wedding in Cana*
Jesus	Abraham	Moses	Jesus
Pontius Pilate	Lot	Pharaoh	Bride and Groom
Disciples	Lot's family	Aaron	Mary
Mary			Disciples

Jesus Walks on Water	*Fall of Jericho*	*Jesus Brings Lazarus Back to Life*
Jesus	Joshua	Jesus
Peter	The seven priets	Lazarus
Disciples		Mary and Martha

5. Jordan, Red Sea, or Sea of Galilee

Objective: To recognize what took place at or near these bodies of water.

Materials Needed: Chalkboard.

The Activity: Write the headings, *Jordan, Red Sea,* and *Sea of Galilee* on the board. Read your prepared statements about these places and ask the children to tell where they took place by naming one of the headings. *Examples:*

1. The Children of Israel crossed it on dry ground. (Red Sea)
2. Jesus got in a boat here and preached. (Sea of Galilee)
3. John baptized Jesus here. (Jordan)
4. Jesus calmed a storm. (Sea of Galilee)
5. The city of Capernaum was near this place. (Sea of Galilee)
6. The Sinai peninsula touches this sea. (Red Sea)

6. Inland or Ports

Objective: To recognize which cities of the Bible are ports or inland.

Materials Needed: Bibles with a map.

The Activity: Have a list of cities prepared before class which include port cities and inland cities. Providing you have maps for the children, you may include cities around the Mediterranean Sea instead of just Palestine. Give the name of the city and children must tell if it is a *port* city or an *inland* city. Try this later without maps. *Examples:*

Port Cities	*Inland Cities*
Sidon	Bethlehem
Tyre	Jerusalem
Caesarea	Nazareth
Joppa	Jericho
Athens	Sychar
Alexandria	Bethany
Capernaum	Emmaus

7. I Visited . . .

Objective: To associate an event with the Biblical city.

Materials Needed: None.

The Activity: Prepare a list of Biblical cities with which one can easily associate a Bible event. Tell the children you will give the name of a city and they are to respond with an event which took place there. *Examples:* The teacher says, "I visited . . .

1. Jerusalem (The Feast of the Passover took place there.)
2. Nazareth (Jesus' hometown.)
3. Bethany (Jesus brought Lazarus back to life.)
4. Nain (Jesus brought the widow's son back to life.)
5. Capernaum (Jesus healed the centurion's servant.)
6. Bethlehem (Jesus was born there.)

8. I Wish to Know

Objective: To review what took place in selected Bible places, not cities.

Materials Needed: None, although a Bible dictionary may be useful.

The Activity: Divide your class into two groups. A student from Group I begins by saying, "I wish to know more about _____." A student from Group II must
(place)
answer by telling one identifying fact about that place. Change the groups around after several turns. *Examples:*

Group I

I wish to know more about:

1. Mount Nebo
2. Mount Sinai
3. Sea of Galilee
4. Gethsemane
5. Red Sea
6. Aijalon

Group II

1. Moses saw the Promised Land.
2. God gave the Ten Commandments.
3. Jesus stilled a storm.
4. Jesus prayed and sweat drops of blood.
5. Israel crossed over on dry land.
6. The moon stood still for Joshua.

9. Where Did They Meet?

Objective; To give practice in associating Bible people with places.

Materials Needed: None.

The Activity: Tell the children that you will give the names of people who met at specific places as recorded in the Bible. Ask them to tell where the people met each other. *Examples:*

1. Jesus and the Samaritan woman (Jacob's Well, or a well)
2. Jesus and John the Baptist (Jordan River area)
3. Gabriel and Mary (her home in Nazareth)
4. Adam and Eve (Garden of Eden)
5. Joseph and his brothers after he was sold (Egypt)
6. The two spies and Rahab (Jericho)
7. Ruth and Boaz (field near Bethlehem)
8. The Marys and the angel on Easter morning (the tomb)
9. Jesus and Zacchaeus (Jericho or sycamore tree)
10. Jesus and the widow (temple or Nain)

10. Another Name

Objective: To give practice in stating Bible names quickly.

Materials Needed: None.

The Activity: Explain to the children that you will give them a Bible name (person or place). After you speak the name someone in the group is to give another name beginning with the same letter as yours. The child who thinks of it first should raise his hand, and state the word. Then he has the opportunity of saying another word and someone else must think of a word which begins with the same letter. *Examples:*

1. Jesus (John, Jairus)
2. Matthew (Miriam, Moab)
3. Ruth (Rachel, Rome)
4. Adam (Aaron, Ahab)
5. Gideon (Golgotha, Gabriel)
6. Lebanon (Lystra, Lazarus)
7. Nineveh (Noah, Nazareth)
8. Simeon (Samaria, Solomon)
9. Timothy (Titus, Tiberius)
10. Babylon (Bethel, Bethany)

11. What's Wrong with the Location?

Objective: To give practice in correctly locating Bible places.

Materials Needed: Chalkboard.

The Activity: Place a rough sketch of the Holy Land map on the board. Write in cities which are located in the correct place, and some which are not in the correct location. Ask your students to tell you what's wrong with the location of the cities or geographical features. *Examples:*

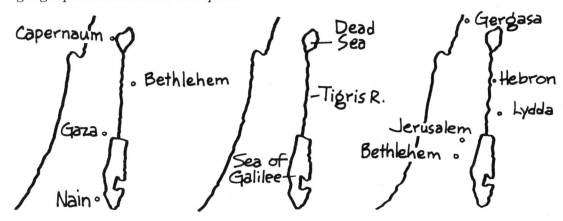

12. Going to Bible Places

Objective: To review approximate locations of Bible places.

Materials Needed: Outline maps of Palestine, pencil colors or crayons, pencils.

The Activity: Give each student a plain outline map of Palestine and several different-colored crayons. The teacher says, "I am going from Capernaum to Jerusalem. Trace the route in blue." They are to label Capernaum and Jerusalem, and trace the route in blue. For each route use a different color. After giving about five trips, have volunteers explain the routes on your classroom map. *Examples:* (1) Nazareth—Bethlehem; (2) Hebron—Gaza; (3) Tyre—Jericho; (4) Mount Nebo—Sea of Galilee; (5) Shechem—Beersheba.

13. Bible Geography

Objective: To help children remember geographical names in the Bible.

Materials Needed: None.

The Activity: Divide the class into two groups. A student from Group I begins the activity by giving the name of a geographical place. A member of Group II must now give the name of a geographical place which begins with the last letter of Group I's name. If a group cannot think of a place, or if they answer incorrectly, the other side scores a point. The scoring side then begins again. Scoring is made *only* when the opposite side cannot think of a name or a correct name. *Examples:* Group I begins with Bethlehem. Group II now gives a geographical name beginning with "m," the last letter in Bethlehem.

Group I	Group II
Bethlehem	Moab
Bethel	Lydda
Aijalon	Nain
Nazareth	Hebron; etc.

14. How Far Is It?

Objective: To become familiar with distances between Bible cities.

Materials Needed: Individual maps with a scale of miles (usually found in the back of most Bibles) and rulers.

The Activity: Explain to the children that they will be finding distances between cities mentioned in the Bible. Ask them to measure the distance with a ruler, and then change it to miles from the scale of miles found on the Bible map. *Examples:*

1. Nazareth—Capernaum (23 miles)
2. Jerusalem—Jericho (14 miles)
3. Nazareth—Jerusalem (70 miles)
4. Bethlehem—Jerusalem (8 miles)
5. Sychar—Bethel (20 miles)
6. Gaza—Jerusalem (48 miles)

15. Bible Quiz—Game 1

Objective: To gain skill in recognizing Bible people and animals.

Materials Needed: None.

The Activity: Ask for two volunteers to come forward. Flip a coin and the one who guesses correctly has the choice of choosing the category—either Bible People or Bible Animals. The other child must take the remaining category. Tell the children you will ask questions, and they must answer each one correctly to stay in the game. When one child cannot continue, ask for another volunteer and so on. The one who stays in the game the longest is the winner. The new volunteer coming into the game has the choice of category. *Examples:*

Questions for Bible People Category

1. Which disciple took care of Jesus' mother? (John)
2. The only woman judge of Israel. (Deborah)
3. He dreamed of a ladder reaching to heaven. (Jacob)
4. The husband of Mary. (Joseph)
5. The great-grandmother of King David. (Ruth)

Questions for Bible Animals

1. Samson tore this animal apart. (lion)
2. The Wise Men rode these animals. (camel)
3. Jonah was in the belly of this animal three days. (whale)
4. Jesus rode into Jerusalem on Palm Sunday on one of these. (donkey)
5. What animals licked the sores of poor Lazarus? (dogs)

Be sure that you have plenty of questions ready for your class. A Bible dictionary and concordance will help you.

16. Bible Quiz—Game 2

Objective: To gain skill in recognizing Bible cities and bodies of water.

Materials Neded: None.

The Activity: Ask for two volunteers to come forward. Flip a coin and the one who guesses correctly has the choice of choosing the category—either Bible Cities or Bodies of Water. The other child must take the remaining category. Tell the children you will ask questions, and they must answer correctly to stay in the game. When one child cannot continue, ask for another volunteer, and so on. The one who stays in the game the longest is the winner. The new volunteer coming into the game has the choice of category. *Examples:*

Questions for Bible Cities Category

1. The city where the temple was located. (Jerusalem)
2. The city where Mary, Martha, and Lazarus lived. (Bethany)

3. In what city was the apostle Paul born? (Tarsus)
4. Jesus' hometown. (Nazareth)
5. The city where the walls came tumbling down. (Jericho)

Questions for Bible Bodies of Water

1. A body of water with no outlet. (Dead Sea)
2. The river in which John baptized Jesus. (Jordan)
3. A brook close to Gethsemane. (Kidron)
4. The sea where the disciples fished. (Sea of Galilee)
5. One of the rivers which flowed through the Garden of Eden. (Tigris or Euphrates)

This type of exercise will lend itself to many other categories, such as Bible Men and Women, Bible Plants and Bible Birds, etc.

17. Choose a Bible Friend

Objective: To discern between Bible people who were good to have for friends, and those who were not.

Materials Needed: None.

The Activity: Prepare a list of Bible people including some who would have been good friends and some who would not have been good friends. Tell the children that you will give a Bible person's name, and they are to decide if they would have chosen him to be a friend or not. Be sure to ask why they made their choice. *Examples:*

1. King Saul (No)	5. Jonathan (Yes)	9. Delilah (No)
2. Moses (Yes)	6. Esther (Yes)	10. Pharaoh (No)
3. Martha (Yes)	7. John (Yes)	11. Herod (No)
4. Pilate (No)	8. Timothy (Yes)	12. Samuel (Yes)

18. Put On Your Thinking Caps

Objective: To give practice in recalling Bible words.

Materials Needed: Chalkboard, paper, pencils.

The Activity: Write one of the letters on the chalkboard and ask the children to list as many Bible words as they can which begin with that letter. Decide on a number to limit the list such as 5 or 10. The student who first lists that number of words is the winner, and must read his list. Now he suggests a letter to the group. A concordance will help to settle any arguments. *Examples:*

A	G	S
Aaron	Gethsemane	Saul
Abel	glory	Syria
Abraham	Gideon	scourge
Absalom	generations	Sabbath
altar	God	sinners

19. Miracles and Parables

Objective: To be better able to recognize Bible narratives which are parables and miracles of Jesus.

Materials Needed: Chalkboard, paper, and pencils.

The Activity: Divide your class into two groups. Assign the heading "Miracles" to one group, and "Parables" to the other. Tell the children they are to list Bible narratives under the assigned heading. The group thinking of the most narratives wins. An alternate way is to ask each child to list as many narratives under both headings as they can. You may want to reward the winner(s) with a tract or gummed seals. *Examples:*

Miracles	*Parables*
Wedding in Cana of Galilee	The Sower
Jesus Stilling the Storm	The Unmerciful Servant
Healing the Ten Lepers	The Lost Sheep
Bringing Jairus' Daughter to Life	The Prodigal Son
The Young Man of Nain	The Ten Maidens
Peter's Catch of Fish	The Weeds among the Wheat
Raising of Lazarus	The Great Supper

20. What Was Their Work?

Objective: To know more about occupations of Bible characters.

Materials Needed: None.

The Activity: Prepare a list of Bible people whose occupation you know. A Bible dictionary will help you in this preparation. Give one of the names to your class and ask a volunteer to tell the occupation of that person. You may divide the class into groups, and tally the results on the chalkboard. *Examples:*

1. Peter (fisherman)
2. Paul (tentmaker and missionary)
3. Zechariah (priest)
4. Luke (physician)
5. Isaiah (prophet)
6. Lydia (sold cloth and dyed goods)
7. Demetrius (silversmith)
8. David, Solomon (king)
9. Habakkuk (prophet)
10. Zacchaeus (tax collector)

21. Who Said It?

Objective: To remember phrases and verses from the Bible.

Materials Needed: None.

The Activity: Prepare a list of selected Bible verses or phrases. Tell the children that you are going to say a verse or phrase from the Bible, and they are to tell who said it. An optional way is to ask the children to select some verses or phrases, and each one presents them to the class. Let them use their Bibles to do this activity, if necessary. *Examples:* (RSV)

1. "You are the Christ, the Son of the living God." (Peter, Matthew 16:16)
2. "Because I live, you will live also." (Jesus, John 14:19)
3. "Behold the Lamb of God." (John the Baptist, John 1:29)
4. "Oh let not the Lord be angry . . . suppose ten are found there." (Abraham, Genesis 18:32)
5. "Lord, now lettest Thou Thy servant depart in peace . . ." (Simeon, Luke 2:29)
6. "Father, I have sinned against heaven . . ." (Prodigal Son, Luke 15:21)

22. The Bible Says So, I Believe It

Objective: To receive practice in recognizing correct quotes of Bible verses.

Materials Needed: None.

The Activity: Explain to the children that you will quote a Bible verse beginning with the words, "The Bible says so." Tell them that you may quote it correctly or incorrectly. If the verse is quoted correctly they are to respond with the words, "I believe it." If the verse is quoted incorrectly they are to remain silent. You may want to divide the class into groups and keep score. When verses are stated incorrectly be sure to ask for the correct wording before proceeding to the next verse. *Examples:* (RSV)

1. "Be faithful unto death, and I will give you the crown of life." Revelation 2:10 (Child answers, "I believe it.")
2. "Because *you* live, *I* will live also." John 14:19 (Children remain silent.)
3. "The blood of Jesus *our* Son cleanses *Him* from all sin." 1 John 1:7 (Remain silent.)
4. "This is the love of God, that we keep His commandments." 1 John 5:3 (I believe it.)
5. "You shall worship the Lord your God and Him only shall you serve." Matthew 4:10 (I believe it.)

23. Question Box

Objective: To review common Bible facts.

Materials Needed: 3″ x 5″ cards, pencils.

The Activity: Write Bible fact questions on the 3″ x 5″ cards. Place the cards in a box and ask the students to draw out one card and answer the question. Have enough cards so each will get at least two turns. *Examples:*

1. Who was the oldest man recorded in the Bible? (Methuselah)
2. A brother of Miriam and Moses. (Aaron)
3. A lady who never had a mother. (Eve)
4. The Alpha and Omega. (Jesus)
5. The daughter-in-law of Naomi (Ruth and Orpah)

24. Prophet, Priest, or King

Objective: To become more aware of the activities of a prophet, priest, and king.

Materials Needed: None.

The Activity: Review with your class the Biblical activities of a prophet, priest, and king. Then ask the children to answer your questions with one of the words "prophet," "priest," or "king." An alternate way to use this activity is for you to prepare a list of names, and have the class tell whether the person named was a prophet, priest, or king. *Examples:*

1. Who would have offered your sacrifice? (priest)
2. You need to convey some important information about an enemy nation. (king)
3. You wish to know more about one of God's commands. (prophet and priest)
4. You wish to know more about a Sabbath regulation. (priest)
5. You want to study more about prayer. (prophet and priest)
6. He is telling people about a future event. (prophet)
7. You want to show your friends the palace. (king)
8. Saul was the first _____ . (king)

Examples for alternate form:

1. Isaiah (prophet)
2. Melchizedek (priest)
3. Josiah (king)
4. David (king)

5. Elijah (prophet)
6. Zechariah (priest)
7. Caiaphas (priest)
8. Jesus (prophet, priest, king)

25. Remember Me?

Objective: To help students review Bible characters.

Materials Needed: Strips of construction paper (white) about 4″ high, liquid pens, pencils.

The Activity: Give each student two or three strips of construction paper and a liquid pen. Assign two or three Bible characters, secretly, to each child. Now ask them to write that name on one side of the card with the liquid pen, and on the other side write an identifying statement about the character. Make certain each one does his own work; let them ask you for help if needed. When all are finished they may take turns holding their flash cards before the class, and ask the others to identify the person on the card. Use them often for review. *Examples:*

1. Lazarus (Jesus brought him back to life.)
2. Nicodemus (Came to Jesus by night.)
3. Solomon (Built the temple.)
4. Noah (Built the ark.)
5. Deborah (Was one of the judges.)

26. Who and What

Objective: To identify people of the Bible.

Materials Needed: None.

The Activity: Prepare a list of Bible people. Divide the class into two groups, one being the "Who's" group and the other the "What's" group. Write a Bible person's name on the chalkboard. One person from the Who's group will give an identifying who statement, and one person from the What's group will give an identifying what-he-did statement. If a group cannot answer correctly, the other side receives the point. *Examples:*

Who's	*What's*
1. Peter—a disciple of Jesus	He denied Jesus.
2. Zechariah—a priest	He doubted God, and became dumb.
3. David—son of Jesse, a king	He killed Goliath.
4. Thomas—a disciple of Jesus	He doubted Jesus was alive.
5. Sarah—Abraham's wife	She doubted God's promise.

27. Bible Synonyms

Objective: To recall sentences from well-known Bible verses, and substitute the correct synonym for the indicated word.

Materials Needed: None.

The Activity: Say the following to the children: "I am going to read a sentence from the Bible. The sentence has one word in it which is not found in the Bible. I will tell you what word it is. Put on your thinking caps and think of the synonym, found in the Bible, which should be used. Listen closely!" *Examples:* (RSV)

"<u>Look</u> and you will find."—seek (Matthew 7:7)
"He who is coming after Me is <u>greater</u> than I."—mightier (Matthew 3:11)
"In the beginning God <u>made</u> the heavens and the earth."—created (Genesis 1:1)
"The whole congregation . . . of Israel <u>complained</u>."—murmured (Exodus 16:2)
"In those days an <u>order</u> went out from Caesar Augustus."—decree (Luke 2:1)
"God so loved the world that He <u>sent</u> His only Son."—gave (John 3:16)
"Go therefore and make <u>followers</u> of all nations."—disciples (Matthew 28:19)

28. Furniture in Bible Homes

Objective: To learn more of how homes in Bible times were furnished.

Materials Needed: Paper and pencils, chalkboard.

The Activity: Ask the children to suggest items of furniture which they know were used in Bible times. Place these on the chalkboard as they are given. Then give each child paper and a pencil and ask them to sketch a floor plan of a Bible home. Now tell them to arrange the furniture by indicating where they would place it on their sketch. *Examples:* (A copy of *Home Life in Bible Times*—St. Louis: Concordia Publishing House—would prove helpful.) Your list may include: Mats, rugs, beds, chairs, stoves or braziers, couch, stools, lamps, candlesticks, the millstone, kneading troughs, and waterpots.

29. Chalkboard Fun

Objective: To identify certain Bible stories from simple sketches.

Materials Needed: None, except the chalkboard.

The Activity: Ask the children to think of a simple way to sketch a Bible story they know well. They may draw a simple sketch on scratch paper, and when it is their turn, they are to sketch it on the chalkboard. After the sketch is finished the other children will guess the title of the Bible story. Each child who wants to should be given an opportunity. *Examples:*

Jesus Dies for Us

Jesus Walks on the Water

Giving of the Law

Easter

Christmas

30. Bible Nouns

Objective: To become more aware of Bible words which must be capitalized.

Materials Needed: Chalkboard.

The Activity: Explain to the children that you will list some Bible nouns on the chalkboard. They are to tell if they are common or proper nouns. A proper noun must be capitalized. An alternate way is to have the children prepare lists for the group. *Examples:*

> christian—Children will answer: Proper with capital "C."
> nation—Children will answer: Common.
> sea of galilee—Proper, capital "S" and "G."
> generation—Common.
> damascus—Proper with capital "D."
> priest—Common.
> Jesus or any divine name—Proper, always capitalized.

31. Foods of Bible Times

Objective: To acquaint children with various foods of the Bible.

Materials Needed: Chalkboard, paper, pencils.

The Activity: Make a list of foods mentioned in the Bible. A good source to use is *Home Life in Bible Times*. Place your list of foods on the chalkboard. Now ask the children to plan a menu for breakfast, lunch, and dinner for a family who lived in Bible times. Share the menus with the class. *Examples:* wheat bread, barley cakes, eggs, milk, butter, cheese, honey, locusts, wine, fish, mutton, lentils, beans, olives, grapes, melons, apples, mint, and figs.

32. Plants of the Bible

Objective: To remember events or people associated with plants of the Bible.

Materials Needed: Bibles, slips of paper.

The Activity: Using a concordance, compile a list of plants with their Biblical reference. Write the references on slips of paper. Give one to each child and have them look up the reference. Children now share with the class the event, parable, or person with which the plant is associated. *Examples:*

1. Luke 19:4—sycamore tree (Zacchaeus climbed it to see Jesus).
2. Matthew 6:28—lilies (Jesus in the Sermon on the Mount).

3. Song of Solomon 2:1—rose (Jesus is called the Rose of Sharon.)
4. Matthew 24:32—fig tree (parable of the Fig Tree).
5. 1 Kings 19:4-5—broom (KJV: juniper) (Elijah was sad and sat under the broom tree).
6. Genesis 8:11—olive (the dove returned with an olive leaf.)
7. Numbers 13:23—grapes (the spies returned with a large cluster of grapes).
8. Genesis 25:34—lentils (Jacob gave Esau the lentils).

33. Plants and Animals Bible Stories

Objective: To recall which Bible narratives mention plants and animals.

Materials Needed: None.

The Activity: Prepare a list of Bible narratives which mention plants and animals. Divide your class into two groups and call one group "Plants" and the other "Animals." Tell the children to choose a writer who will list all the narratives for the group. The "Plants" group should list Bible stories which mention plants, and the "Animals" group will list Bible stories which mention animals. The group with the most wins. Use your list to help get them started. *Examples:*

Plants	*Animals*
Naboth's Vineyard	Daniel in the Lions' Den
Ruth	Jonah and the Whale
Joseph in Egypt	Absalom's Rebellion
Joseph's Dream	Samson Kills a Lion
Parable of the Sower	Draught of Fishes
Sermon on the Mount	The Lost Sheep
Jesus Enters Jerusalem	Offering of Isaac
Creation	Creation

34. Bible Animals

Objective: To recognize animals and events of the Bible.

Materials Needed: Paper and pencils.

The Activity: Write the names of Bible animals on slips of paper and give one to each child. A concordance will help you locate Bible animals. Ask the children to identify a Bible event or statement with which the animal is associated. *Examples:*

1. donkey (Jesus rode on one as He entered Jerusalem.)
2. camel (The Wise Men.)
3. sheep (Parable of the Lost Sheep.)

4. lamb (Jesus is called Lamb of God.)
5. locusts (Plagues in Egypt.)
6. leopards (Can the leopard change his spots? Jer. 13:23.)

35. Name the Bible Bird

Objective: To recognize birds of the Bible.

Materials Needed: Bibles, paper, pencils, concordance.

The Activity: Make use of a concordance to find Bible references which name different kinds of birds. Write the references on slips of paper, one reference on each. Have each child draw a slip "out of the hat." Now ask the children to research their reference and then write one clue about the bird mentioned in their reference. When all are finished, each child reads his clue to the class, and the students guess the name of the bird. They may then share the message of the Bible verse. *Examples:*

1. Matthew 10:29-31 (sparrows)
2. Psalm 84:3 (swallow and sparrow)
3. Genesis 8:7 (raven)
4. Genesis 8:10-11 (dove)
5. 1 Kings 17:6 (raven)
6. Luke 2:22-24 (turtledove and pigeon)
7. Psalm 103:5 (eagle)
8. Isaiah 40:31 (eagle)
9. Job 39:26 (hawk)
10. Job 39:13-14 (ostrich)

36. Weather Phenomena

Objective: To become aware of weather phenomena mentioned in the Bible, and to realize that God controls weather.

Materials Needed: Bibles, paper, pencils, concordance.

The Activity: Using the concordance, prepare a list of Bible references which speak of weather phenomena. Have the children draw a reference "out of the hat," look it up, and write one clue about the weather phenonenon. When all are finished, each child reads the clues and the others guess what it is. Ask them to tell how the verse shows God controls the weather, if it does. *Examples:*

1. Job 38:22-23 (snow and hail)
2. Psalm 135:7 (lightning and rain)
3. Job 5:10 (rain)
4. Matthew 5:45 (rain)
5. Psalm 147:8 (rain)
6. Psalm 147:16 (snow and frost)
7. Psalm 147:18 (wind)
8. Job 38:28 (dew and rain)
9. Luke 8:25 (wind)
10. Psalm 107:29 (storms)

37. Finish the Bible Verse

Objective: To review and learn well-chosen Bible verses.

Materials Needed: None.

The Activity: Explain to the children that you will state the beginning phrases of certain Bible verses which they have learned. Volunteers are to finish the verses. *Examples:*

"God so loved the world that He . . ." (John 3:16)
"By grace you have been saved through faith; and this is . . ." (Eph. 2:8-9)
"Go therefore and make disciples of all nations . . ." (Matt. 28:19)
"Blessed rather are those who hear . . ." (Luke 11:28)
"In the beginning God . . ." (Genesis 1:1)

38. Bible Money

Objective: To recognize different forms of money used in Bible times.

Materials Needed: None, although a Bible dictionary may be handy.

The Activity: Read the following questions to your class. Ask that volunteers answer with a form of money mentioned in the Bible. *Examples:*

1. For how much did Judas betray Jesus? (30 pieces of silver)
2. How much did the widow place into the treasury of the temple? (two copper coins [KJV: mites])
3. How much money did the disciples say they needed to feed the 5,000? (200 denarii [KJV: pennyworth])
4. How much did the Good Samaritan pay to help the wounded Jew? (two denarii [KJV: pence])
5. In the parable of the Unmerciful Servant how much did he owe his master? (10,000 talents)
6. How much money did Naaman take with him to give to Elijah? (ten talents of silver, 6,000 shekels [KJV pieces] of gold)
7. In the parable how much did the nobleman give to each servant to invest? (10 pounds)

39. Person, Place, or Object

Objective: To give practice in naming Bible people, places, or objects.

Materials Needed: Spinner labeled with letters of the alphabet.

The Activity: Construct a spinner from poster board, and label the outer ring with the letters of the alphabet. The arrow can be fastened loosely with a paper fastener. Ask the children to choose a category—person, place, or object—and then to take turns spinning. They must then give the name of a Bible person, place or object beginning with the letter(s) at which the arrow stopped. *Examples:*

Persons	*Places*	*Objects*
Adam	Galilee	mercy seat
Benjamin	Hebron	nets
Caiaphas	Jerusalem	olive
Deborah	Kidron	pearl
Eli	Lydda	robe

40. Kings, Women, or Prophets

Objective: To quickly name kings, women, or prophets of the Bible.

Materials Needed: Spinner labeled kings, women, and prophets.

The Activity: Construct a spinner from poster board and label the outer ring with the words "kings," "women," and "prophets." The arrow can be fastened loosely with a paper fastener. Children take turns spinning, and must give the name of a Bible person for the category at which the arrow stops. *Examples:*

Kings	*Women*	*Prophets*
Saul	Mary	Isaiah
David	Martha	Jeremiah
Solomon	Deborah	Elijah
Hezekiah	Priscilla	Daniel
Josiah	Ruth	Micah

41. Whose Father or Mother

Objective: To know fathers and mothers of Bible characters.

Materials Needed: Bible dictionary or concordance.

The Activity: Prepare a list of people mentioned in the Bible for whom you know their father or mother. Give the children one of the names and ask them to tell who the father or mother of that person is. You may also reverse the game by giving the names of the parents, and the students respond with the names of the children. *Examples:*

1. Joseph (father was Jacob)
2. Isaac (father was Abraham) (mother was Sarah)
3. David (father was Jesse)
4. Solomon (father was David) (mother was Bathsheba)
5. Cain and Abel (parents were Adam, Eve)
6. Adam and Eve (had no father or mother)
7. Obed (mother was Ruth)
8. Jesus (Mary was His mother)

42. Who's the Main Character?

Objective: To recall Bible narratives and tell the main character of each.

Materials Needed: None.

The Activity: Prepare a list of Bible narratives familiar to your class. Ask the children to tell the main character in each narrative that you will describe or name for them. *Examples:*

1. The Flood (Noah)
2. The Ten Lepers (Jesus)
3. Sermon on the Mount (Jesus)
4. The Golden Calf (Aaron)
5. Israel in the Wilderness (Moses)
6. The Fall of Jericho (Joshua)
7. Building of the Temple (Solomon)
8. Stilling of the Tempest (Jesus)

43. My Favorite Bible City

Objective: To recall facts of Bible cities.

Materials Needed: Chalkboard, reference books, facsimilie airline tickets.

The Activity: Place the following statement on the chalkboard: Finish this

statement in 25 words or less: "My favorite city of the Bible is _____

because _____ .

Children are to finish the statement and share it with the class. Reward them when finished with a facsimile airline ticket to that city. *Examples:* Include such cities as Jerusalem, Nazareth, Capernaum, Bethlehem, and Bethany.

44. Whose City?

Objective: To help children associate people with Bible cities.

Materials Needed: None.

The Activity: Prepare a list of cities mentioned in the Bible. The teacher calls out the name of a city, and children answer with a person(s) most often associated with that city. *Examples:* Bethany (Mary, Martha, Lazarus); Jericho (Joshua); Jerusalem (Solomon—temple); Nineveh (Jonah); Nazareth (Joseph, Mary, Jesus); Bethlehem (Jesus); Sychar (Samaritan woman); Capernaum (Jesus, centurion); Tyre and Sidon (Canaanite woman); Emmaus (Cleopas and friend); Tarsus (Saul or Paul).

45. What's the Message?

Objective: To gain practice in interpreting Bible verses.

Materials Needed: Bible for each child, chalkboard.

The Activity: Prepare a list of Bible references which give a clear message. The selected verses need not be familiar references, although the first one should be. Write the reference on the board and ask the children to locate it in their Bible. After reading and thinking about it, they are to tell what message God gives us in that verse(s). You may want to use obvious ones for your slower students. *Examples:*

1. "He died for all, that those who live might live no longer for themselves but for Him who for their sake died and was raised." 2 Corinthians 5:15 (Jesus died for us; let's live for Him)
2. "He who endures to the end will be saved." Matthew 24:13 (Remain faithful to Jesus always)
3. "Call upon Me in the day of trouble; I will deliver you, and you shall glorify Me." Psalm 50:15 (Ask God to help you; don't forget to say "thank you")
4. "Through love be servants of one another." Galatians 5:13 (God wants us to help each other)

46. I Spent the Day With . . .

Objective: To imagine what it must have been like in Bible times.

Materials Needed: Paper and pencils.

The Activity: Ask children to choose a Bible character and describe three things that happened on a day spent with that person. Share the short paragraphs with each other. *Examples:* David, Noah, Moses, Children of Israel in the Wilderness, Jonah, Esther, Ruth, Jesus, and Paul.

47. Old or New Testament Events

Objective: To review Bible events and to identify whether Old or New Testament.

Materials Needed: None.

The Activity: Prepare a list of events (narratives) from the Bible. Ask your students to tell when the events took place, during the Old or New Testament. Depend on "Scouts Honor" as children tally their own correct answers. *Examples:*

1. Feeding of the Five Thousand (NT)
2. Jesus Stills the Storm (NT)
3. Creation (OT)
4. Stephen is Martyred (NT)
5. Solomon Builds the Temple (OT)
6. Naboth's Vineyard (OT)
7. The Ten Lepers (NT)
8. Paul's Journey (NT)
9. Queen Esther (OT)
10. Daniel in the Lions' Den (OT)

48. Old or New Testament Places

Objective: To associate places mentioned in the Bible with the Old or New Testament.

Materials Needed: None.

The Activity: Prepare a list of places found primarily in the Old Testament, and some found in the New Testament. The children are to tell if the place you give is associated mainly with the Old or New Testament Bible history. *Examples:*

1. Babylon (OT)
2. Bethany (NT)
3. Capernaum (NT)
4. Ur (OT)
5. Lystra (NT)
6. Nazareth (NT)
7. Mount Hermon (OT)
8. Mount Sinai (OT)
9. Shiloh (OT)
10. Emmaus (NT)

49. Identify the Bible Book—Old Testament

Objective: To become better acquainted with the books of the Old Testament.

Materials Needed: None.

The Activity: Prepare questions about the books of the Old Testament, and ask the children to identify the book. *Examples:*

1. Name the first book in the Old Testament, and Bible. (Genesis)
2. Name the last book of the Old Testament. (Malachi)

3. Which books are called the Pentateuch (Genesis, Exodus, Leviticus, Numbers, Deuteronomy)
4. Which book contains the creation account? (Genesis)
5. Name one of the books of the prophets (Joel, etc.)

50. Identify the Bible Book—New Testament

Objective: To become better acquainted with the books of the New Testament.

Materials Needed: None.

The Activity: Prepare questions about the books of the New Testament, and ask the children to identify the book. *Examples:*

1. Which book of the Bible comes after John? (Acts)
2. Which is the first book of the New Testament? (Matthew)
3. The book which contains the familiar Christmas story. (Luke)
4. Which books are called the gospels? (Matthew, Mark, Luke, John)
5. Name one of the epistles of Paul. (Ephesians, etc.)

51. How Did They Do It?

Objective: To appreciate how work or recreation was done in Bible times.

Materials Needed: None, although *Home Life in Bible Times*, published by Concordia Publishing House, will help you.

The Activity: Consult the booklet, *Home Life in Bible Times* or one similar, and prepare a list of occupations and forms of recreation. Ask your students to tell how these actions were done. Do not expect complete explanations. You will want to add to their comments. *Examples:* fishing, playing music, baking, cooking, threshing grain, grinding flour, and carrying water.

52. How Was Life Different?

Objective: To learn more of how Bible people lived.

Materials Needed: Paper and pencils.

The Activity: Hand out paper and pencils to your students, and ask them to make two headings on the paper, "Today" and "Bible Times." Tell them to list different ways of life under the column "Today," and then to tell how the way of life existed in Bible times. Share the findings in a class discussion. *Examples:*

Today	Bible Times
1. electric lights	oil lamps
2. driving cars	walking or donkeys
3. gas heat	coals in braziers
4. television	visiting, etc.
5. newspapers	messengers
6. running water	water jars
7. automatic washers	wash by hand
8. school buses	walked to synagog schools

53. Bible Words Review

Objective: To review selected words from the Bible.

Materials Needed: 3″ x 5″ cards on which the teacher has written Bible words.

The Activity: Prepare enough Bible word cards so that each child will have three, and at the same time record a master list from which you will dictate the definitions. After each child has received his three word cards, call out the definition to one of the words. The child who has the correct word cards stands and reads the word. Continue until all cards are used. *Examples:*

1. A word which means a follower of Jesus. (Disciple)
2. A word which means our sins are canceled. (Forgiveness)
3. God made the heavens and earth. (Creation)
4. The good news of heaven. (Gospel)
5. The undeserved love of God. (Grace)
6. A heart to heart talk with God. (Prayer)

7. Eternal
8. Faith
9. Kingdom
10. Forgive
11. Sin
12. Salvation

54. Bible Alphabet

Objective: To quickly think of Bible nouns.

Materials Needed: Paper and pencils.

The Activity: Ask your class to write the letters of the alphabet on paper in a column, but do not include "x." Tell them to think of a Bible *noun* that begins with each letter, but not to include articles and pronouns. An option would be to limit the words to people, but then leave out w, x, and y. The first one to finish is the winner and receives a tract. *Examples:* A-Adam, B-Benjamin, C-Cain, D-Deborah, E-Eve, F-faith, G-God, H-Hannah, I-Immanuel, J-James, K-knowledge, L-love, M-Moriah, N-Nebo, O-Orpah, P-Paul, Q-queen, R-Rachel, S-Saul, T-Timothy, U-Uriah, V-Vashti, W-wilderness, Y-year, Z-Zechariah.

55. Christmas, Lent, Easter

Objective: To associate Bible places and events with the correct season of the church year.

Materials Needed: None.

The Activity: Prepare a list of people, places and events which could be associated with the seasons of the church year. You will give the name of a person, place, or event, and children are to respond with the proper season of the church year—Advent, Lent, Easter, Ascension, Pentecost. *Examples:*

1. Pilate (Lent)
2. Emmaus (Easter)
3. Bethlehem (Christmas)
4. Wise Men (Christmas)
5. Betrayal (Lent)
6. Shepherds (Christmas)
7. Sunday (Easter)
8. Cleopas (Easter)
9. Tomb (Easter)
10. Golgotha (Lent)

56. Numbers from the Bible

Objective: To recognize certain numbers used in the Bible.

Materials Needed: 3″ x 5″ cards, magic marker.

The Activity: Select common numbers used in the Bible, and write them on 3″ x 5″ cards with a magic marker. You may assign numbers to the children and ask them to do this, if you prefer. A card is held before the group, and volunteers tell what person or event is associated with that number. Keep the flash cards, add to them, and reuse again. *Examples.*

1. 2—Noah took two into the ark.
2. 3—Jesus rose after three days.
3. 7—Priests encompassed Jericho seven times.
4. 10—Jesus healed 10 lepers.
5. 5—Five virgins were wise and five foolish.
6. 99—Leave the 99 sheep and look for the lost one.
7. 12—There were 12 tribes.
8. 5,000—Jesus fed 5,000 people.
9. 1—Lord our God is *one* Lord.
10. 40—rained 40 days and nights.

57. Hunting for Bible Treasures

Objective: To give practice in finding words in Bible references from a description.

Materials Needed: Bibles.

The Activity: Prepare a list of Bible references in which the students are to find a word which you will describe. Tell the children to locate the Bible reference and listen to the clue which you will give them. Now they are to find that treasure (word or phrase) from the clue you have given. *Examples:*

1. One who teaches contrary to the Bible. Matthew 7:15—false prophet
2. A word which means a teaching of the Bible. Matthew 15:9—doctrine
3. A phrase which refers to Jesus. John 1:29—Lamb of God
4. One word which means to make holy. Ephesians 5:25-27—sanctify
5. A word which means the unmerited love of God. Ephesians 2:8-9—grace
6. To be sorry for sins. Acts 2:38—repent

58. Who Am I?

Objective: To become more familiar with Bible characters through asking questions.

Materials Needed: Paper, magic marker, stick pins.

The Activity: Prepare a list of Bible people, one for each member of your class. Print the name of the Bible person on paper with a magic marker, and pin one to the *back* of each student. They must not know the name they are given. Tell the children to circulate through the room and ask questions of others which will help them guess their Bible name. They may not ask directly who they are. The first one to guess wins and the others continue until all have guessed who they are. *Examples:* You may want to use such names as: Peter, John, Zacchaeus, Mary, Ruth, Paul, David, Solomon, Joseph, and Sarah.

59. Bible Word Building

Objective: To build words from the letters of selected Bible words.

Materials Needed: Paper and pencils.

The Activity: Devise a list of five or six words from the Bible. Ask the children to build smaller words from the letters found in the word you will write on the board. They should write their list on the paper provided and then read them to the class at the end of the time specified by you. The winner is the one who has the most words, and should receive a tract. *Examples:*

People	Christian	Galatians	Multitude
pop	an	an	lit
lop	Christ	at	mite
peep	ran	ant	mute
hep	rain	sin	time
pole	tan	lag	tide
	hit	tin	mud

60. A Forbidden Word

Objective: To answer questions without using a certain Bible word.

Materials Needed: None.

The Activity: Tell the children that you do not want them to use certain words in answering questions. State the question and ask them to answer the question without using the forbidden word. A student who cannot answer the question or uses the forbidden word is eliminated from the game. Make sure all children receive a turn. *Examples:*

1. Do not use the word Jesus.
   Who died on the cross for you?
   Who is the Son of God?
   Who made Lazarus alive?
   (Use Savior, Redeemer, Christ.)

2. Do not use the word Galilee.
   On what lake did Jesus walk?
   On what lake did the disciples catch many fish?
   What sea is located in nothern Palestine?
   (Use Tiberius or Gennesaret.)

3. Do not use the word Bible.
   Where do you find the creation account?
   Where do we find God's plan of salvation?
   Which book is the best seller?
   Which book is God's Word?
   (Use Scriptures, Holy Writ, Holy Scriptures, etc.)

4. Do no use the word sin.
   What do we call breaking God's law?
   What did Jesus call sins in the Lord's Prayer?
   What did Satan want Adam and Eve to do?
   (Use disobey, transgressions, iniquities.)

Do not use all the questions from each category at once, but mix them up.

61. Jumbled Bible Words

Objective: To gain practice in identifying Bible words from jumbled words.

Materials Needed: Chalkboard.

The Activity: Prepare a list of jumbled Bible words. Tell the children that you will write a jumbled word on the board, and as soon as they recognize it to raise their hand and spell the word correctly. Proceed with other words. Depend on "Scouts Honor" in asking the children to keep tally of the number identified. *Examples:* 1. n a c a (Cana) 2. c s u m i n e d o (Nicodemus) 3. n e r c a u m p a (Capernaum) 4. n o j h (John) 5. t u r h (Ruth) 6. e m a g e n t h e s (Gethsemane) 7. d v a d i (David) 8. y m r a (Mary)

62. Scrambled Bible Verses

Objective: To identify Bible verses.

Materials Needed: Chalkboard, paper, and pencils.

The Activity: Prepare a list of scrambled Bible verses which you know the children have learned. Write the scrambled Bible verse on the board, and ask the students to unscramble the verse by writing the words in the correct order. The child to finish first gets to read the verse to the class. Allow enough time for slower students to complete it. *Examples:*

1. God with nothing be will impossible.
   ("With God nothing will be impossible." Luke 1:37)
2. house every someone builder is things God built by but the all of
   ("Every house is built by someone, but the builder of all things is God." Hebrews 3:4)
3. blood Jesus sin cleanses us of the from all Son His
   ("The blood of Jesus His Son cleanses us from all sin." 1 John 1:7)
4. Christ if creation is new a anyone in is he.
   ("If anyone is in Christ, he is a new creation." 2 Corinthians 5:17)
5. I lo always you age close of the the to with am.
   ("Lo, I am with you always, to the close of the age." Matthew 28:20)

63. Bible Pen Pals

Objective: To use imagination in order to enrich certain Bible events.

Materials Needed: Paper and pencils.

The Activity: Ask the children to imagine they are one of the Bible characters you will suggest to them. Tell them to write a letter to you telling what it was like to be a part of one of the events recorded in the Bible. *Example:*

Dear Mrs. Jones,

    I am writing to tell you what it felt like when Jesus brought my brother Lazarus back to life. Martha and I were just so happy we couldn't stop thanking Jesus. It was simply astounding to hear Jesus call out, "Lazarus, come forth," and immediately our brother came walking out of the tomb. I have never seen anything like this before. Jesus is surely the Son of God.

Love,
Mary of Bethany

64. Finish the Bible Story

Objective: To give children practice in telling a Bible narrative in their own words.

Materials Needed: None, unless you ask them to write the story.

The Activity: Make a list of several Bible stories which your class has studied recently. Begin a Bible narrative for them, and ask a volunteer to complete it. Reward those who do with a tract. Examples:

1. A marriage took place in Cana of Galilee. Jesus, Mary, and the disciples were there . . . (A volunteer finishes the story.)
2. Jesus and the disciples were crossing the Sea of Galilee. Jesus was tired and fell asleep in the back of the boat. Suddenly . . .
3. It was Easter morning. The two Mary's and Salome went to the tomb to anoint Jesus' body. When they arrived at the tomb . . .

65. Spelling Bible Words

Objective: To receive practice in spelling common Biblical words.

Materials Needed: Paper and pencils.

The Activity: There are certain Biblical words which every Christian will want to spell correctly. Prepare a list of words from your lessons being studied, or use the examples below. Give your children about 10 words each week, tell them to study at home, and then dictate them to the class the following Sunday or weekday. *Examples:*

Scripture	eternal	disciples	sanctification	faith
Bible	heaven	almighty	Baptism	Apostles' Creed
inspired	mercy	blessed	Communion	Commandments
creation	forgive	glory	Christian	
Law	Father	righteous	resurrection	
Gospel	Jesus	iniquity	Kingdom	
holy	Holy Spirit	redeemed	prayer	

66. Bible Chronology

Objective: To review Bible chronology.

Materials Needed: None.

The Activity: Prepare a list of Bible events and people. Give the name of one of the Bible people or events and ask the students to tell what or who comes after. Use the multiple choice approach and give two events or people to choose from. *Examples:*

Ask what or who comes after—

1. The Baptism of Jesus (<u>Wedding in Cana</u>, Christmas Story)
2. The Fall of Jericho (Noah, <u>Gideon</u>)
3. Jesus Enters Jerusalem (<u>Jesus in Gethsemane</u>, The Ten Lepers)
4. Abraham (<u>Samuel</u>, Cain and Abel)
5. Nicodemus (John the Baptist, <u>Stephen</u>)
6. Easter (<u>Paul's Missionary Journeys</u>, Feeding of the Five Thousand)

67. Beat the Clock

Objective: To motivate children to learn the books of the Bible in order.

Materials Needed: Watch with a secondhand, Bible.

The Activity: Ask the children to take a few moments to review the books of the Bible, taking into consideration they have learned them already. Agree upon a time limit in which your children should be able to say the books of the Bible. Then ask volunteers to beat the clock by saying them faster than the agreed time. Remind children of the reason for memorizing the books of the Bible in order, namely, to locate references quickly. *Example:* Old Testament books could be said in about 35 seconds; New Testament books in 25 seconds. You may set the time limit higher to begin with.

68. Know Your Bible Chapters

Objective: To give practice in recognizing certain chapters of the Bible.

Materials Needed: None.

The Activity: Prepare a list of famous chapters from the Bible, and spend some time familiarizing your class with them. Then ask the students to identify the chapter you will name. *Examples:* You will include:

1. Shepherd Psalm (Psalm 23)
2. Sermon on the Mount (Matthew 5)
3. Creation Chapter (Genesis 1)
4. Christmas Chapter (Luke 2)

5. Ten Commandments (Exodus 20, Deut. 5)
6. Love Chapter (1 Corinthians 13)
7. Citizen Chapter (Romans 13)
8. The Help Psalm (Psalm 121)
9. Prayer Chapter (Luke 11)
10. Heaven Chapter (Revelation 21)
11. Lord's Supper Chapter (1 Corinthians 11
12. Pentecost Chapter (Acts 2)

69. Know the Psalms

Objective: To be able to recognize certain Psalms by their content.

Materials Needed: Bibles.

The Activity: After a sufficient time of teaching children the content of well-selected Psalms, children will be able to recognize the various Psalms by heading and number. Give the Psalm heading and ask children to state the number of the Psalm. You may want to limit your list at first to those indicated in the examples. *Examples:*

1. The Shepherd Psalm—Psalm 23
2. The Repentance Psalm—Psalm 51
3. God's Happy People Psalm—Psalm 1
4. The Praises Psalm—Psalm 111
5. The Help Psalm—Psalm 121
6. The Refuge Psalm—Psalm 46
7. The Psalm of Protection—Psalm 91
8. The Thanksgiving Psalm—Psalm 67
9. The Trust Psalm—Psalm 37

70. In Which Book of the Bible?

Objective: To recognize in which book of the Bible certain references are found. (Alternate—to recognize specific references.)

Materials Needed: Bibles.

The Activity: Prepare a list of Bible verses to read to the class. As you read each verse ask the students to tell in what book of the Bible each verse is found. Reward the top three winners with some tracts to share with others. An alternate way is to have the children give the specific Bible reference. (RSV) *Examples:*

1. "In the beginning God created the heavens and the earth." (Genesis 1:1)
2. "To us a child is born, to us a son is given." (Isaiah 9:6)
3. "But Mary kept all these things, pondering them in her heart." (Luke 2:19)
4. "Why do you seek the living among the dead?" (Luke 24:5)
5. "The Lord is my shepherd, I shall not want." (Psalm 23:1)
6. "The fear of the Lord is the beginning of knowledge." (Proverbs 1:7)
7. "Be faithful unto death, and I will give you the crown of life." (Rev. 2:10)

71. Guess Who

Objective: To identify people of the Bible.

Materials Needed: Slips of paper, pencils, and a small box.

The Activity: Give each child a slip of paper and have them write three clues about a Bible character. After all have finished collect the slips and place them in the box. Shuffle them and ask each child to draw one slip from the box. Tell them they are to write the name of the person being described in the clues on the back of the slip. Now share them and give a tract to those who get them correct. An alternate way of doing this is to ask for one clue only. *Examples:* Clues could be written in this manner:

1. A disciple of Jesus   2. His name means rock   3. He denied Jesus (Peter)
1. A member of the Sanhedrin   2. He came to see Jesus at night   3. He did not understand how one could be born again (Nicodemus)
1. Her sister's name was Mary   2. Her brother was Lazarus   3. Lived in Bethany (Martha)

72. Bible Story Question Cards

Objective: To review facts of Bible stories.

Materials Needed: 3″ x 5″ cards and pencils.

The Activity: Give each child a 3″ x 5″ card. Ask them to illustrate a favorite Bible story from the current quarter using stick people and simple sketches. On the back of the card they are to write three questions about the story. After enough time has been allowed, collect the cards and place them in a box. Now have each person draw one card out of the box. They are to identify the Bible story from the sketch and answer the three questions on the back. You may want to give a tract to those who answer all questions correctly. *Examples:*

1. On what day did Jesus die on the cross?
2. What happened in nature when He died?
3. Who was crucified with Him?

73. The Ten Commandments

Objective: To be aware of the many ways God's law is broken.

Materials Needed: Newspapers, magazines.

The Activity: Ask the children to look through the newspapers and magazines you have provided, and search for articles, or simply headlines, which show that God's law has been broken. After sufficient time ask the children to share with each other a brief resume of the event, and also tell which commandment was broken. The teacher and the class should then recite that commandment together. *Examples:*

1. An article on a shooting. (Fifth Commandment)
2. Article on a bank robbery. (Seventh Commandment)
3. Someone sues for slander. (Eighth Commandment)
4. A person is arrested for child abuse. (Fifth Commandment)

74. Which Commandment?

Objective: To review what the Ten Commandments forbid or require.

Materials Needed: None.

The Activity: Take a few moments to review with your children what the Ten Commandments forbid and require. From your prepared list of actions forbidden by the commandments, ask the children to identify the commandment which forbids the action. An optional way is to have the children ask the questions. *Examples:*

1. Which commandment forbids fraud? (seventh)
2. Cursing? (second)
3. Disobedience to parents and teachers? (fourth)
4. Willfully hurting someone? (fifth)
5. Gossip? (eighth)
6. Placing material things ahead of God? (first)

75. Finish the Commandment

Objective: To be able to recite each of the Ten Commandments.

Materials Needed: Your denomination's catechism.

The Activity: Tell the children that you will say the beginning words of the commandments. Volunteers are to finish the commandment. *Examples:* (Quotes here are from *The Small Catechism, by Martin Luther, in Contemporary English.* You may also use the "What does this mean" part from the same book, if you wish.)

1. You shall not covet your neighbor' s wife . . .
2. Remember the . . .
3. Honor your . . .
4. You shall not commit . . .
5. You shall not bear . . .
6. You shall not . . . (kill or steal)
7. You shall not take . . .
8. You shall have . . .

76. Find the Object

Objective: To give practice in locating Bible references.

Materials Needed: Bibles, chalkboard.

The Activity: Use the prepared list of Bible references below, or compile your own. Write a reference on the chalkboard and ask the children to locate the reference in their Bibles, and find the object (or the owner) which you will describe only briefly. Then proceed with the others in the list. *Examples:*

1. A chest—Numbers 10:33. (Ark of the Covenant)
2. A sword—1 Samuel 17:51. (David's)
3. A chariot—Genesis 50:9. (Joseph's)
4. Arrows—1 Samuel 20:18-20. (Jonathan's)
5. It belonged to David—1 Samuel 17:50. (sling)
6. A coat—Genesis 37:3. (Joseph's)
7. It belonged to Gideon—Judges 7:18. (trumpet)
8. A vineyard—1 Kings 21:1. (Naboth's)
9. A crown—Esther 2:17. (Esther's)
10. Blood money—Matthew 27:9. (Judas')

77. Name the Roman

Objective: To recognize Roman people mentioned in the Bible.

Materials Needed: None.

The Activity: Use the prepared list of Romans below, or make your own. Using a multiple choice approach, ask the students to identify the Roman name in each exercise. *Examples:*

1. (John, centurion, Micah)
2. (Mary, Mark, Marcus)
3. (Cornelius, Stephen, Joash)
4. (Aijalon, Augustus, Elim)
5. (Edom, Ararat, Caesar)
6. (Publius, Peter, Ruth)
7. (Pilate, Martha, Jesus)
8. (James, Nathaniel, Festus)
9. (Agrippa, Felix, Matthew)
10. (Sergius Paulus, Ruth, Philip)

78. Bible Pictures

Objective: To identify Bible narratives or characters from pictures.

Materials Needed: Bible narrative pictures from the picture file.

The Activity: Go to your picture file and select several pictures which show a scene from a Bible narrative. Tell the children that you will display a picture and they are to identify the Bible narrative. An alternate way is to limit the pictures to Bible people and have the children name the people being displayed. Reward the winners with a mounted picture. *Examples:* If you do not have a picture file, you can find excellent pictures from Sunday school leaflets, bulletin covers, *Ideals* magazines, church periodicals, and coloring books.

79. Bible Word Association

Objective: To associate Bible events or quotations with selected words.

Materials Needed: None.

The Activity: Draw up a list of words with which a Bible event or quotation can be associated. Explain to the children that you will give them a word and they must respond with a Bible event or quotation in which that word was used. *Examples:*

1. lilies—"Consider the lilies of the field . . ."
2. light—"I am the light of the world . . ."
3. write—"Write, for these words are true . . ."
4. walls—The walls of Jericho came tumbling down.
5. bread—Jesus took bread . . . and said, "Take eat . . ."
6. vow—Jacob vowed a vow
7. lamb—"Behold the lamb of God . . ."
8. always—"Lo, I am with you always . . ."
9. blessed—"Blessed rather are those . . ."
10. love—"Love believes all things, hopes all . . ."

80. Find the Key Word

Objective: To give practice in locating Bible verses and using theological words correctly.

Materials Needed: Chalkboard, concordance.

The Activity: Place three Bible references on the chalkboard, all of which have the same word in it. Ask the children to find the key word in the verses. After they have discussed the key word, they are to use the word correctly in a sentence. An alternate way is to have the children suggest verses to the group. The child who first finds the key word in all three verses and uses it correctly in a sentence would give the next 3 references. *Examples:* (RSV)

2 Timothy 3:16			Proverbs 14:5	
John 10:35	} Scripture(s)		Matthew 24:45	} faithful
John 5:39			Matthew 25:21	

Genesis 1:3 Exodus 13:21 Psalm 119:105	} light	Psalm 65:2 Philippians 4:6 Mark 11:24	} prayer	
John 17:17 Ephesians 5:26 Hebrews 13:12	} sanctify	Acts 4:16 Titus 1:3 1 Timothy 3:16	} manifest	

81. Flannelboard Fun

Objective: To identify Bible narratives from scenes.

Materials Needed: Flannelboard and flannel scenes.

The Activity: Ask the nursery or primary teacher if you may use some of the flannelgraph scenes from her department. Divide your class into groups and ask the children in one group to set up a display for a Bible narrative from the sets you have gotten from the nursery teacher. When they are finished, the other groups are to tell what Bible story is illustrated. The group which first guesses the story is it for the next scene. *Examples:* Depends on which scenes are available in your church. Make certain that your children place the flannel scenes back in the right envelope.

82. Objects and People Association

Objective: To associate Bible people with objects mentioned in the Bible.

Materials Needed: None.

The Activity: Prepare a list of Bible objects with which one can readily associate Bible people. Ask the children to associate a Bible person's name with the object stated. *Examples:*

1. Cross (Jesus)
2. Ark (Noah)
3. Sword (Peter, Goliath)
4. Coat of many colors (Joseph)
5. Walls of Jericho (Joshua)
6. Manger (Jesus)
7. Lamps (Ten Maidens)
8. Locusts and wild honey (John the Baptist)
9. Temple (Solomon, Jesus, Simeon)
10. Two tablets of stone (Moses)
11. Water jars (Jesus)
12. Sling (David)

83. Three Questions

Objective: To give practice in recalling Bible people.

Materials Needed: None.

The Activity: Explain to the children that you are thinking of a Bible person, and they are to guess who it is by asking no more than three questions each. As soon as a student uses his three questions without guessing the name correctly, he is out of the game. The student who guesses the name correctly is it for the next game, and will think of a Bible person's name which the others must guess. *Examples:* Suggested questions to ask:

1. Is it a man or woman?
2. Is this person found in the Old or New Testament?
3. Was this person a king or queen, prophet or prophetess, etc.

Suggested names: Peter, Elijah, Moses, Paul, Esther, Mary, and David.

84. Wisdom from Proverbs

Objective: To appreciate the guidance from the book of Proverbs.

Materials Needed: Bibles.

The Activity: Prepare a list of selected verses from the book of Proverbs. Leave out one of the obvious words and ask the children to give the missing word in order to complete the verse. Winners may be rewarded with tracts to share with unchurched friends. *Examples:* (RSV)

1. "The _____ of the Lord is the beginning of knowledge." (1:7)
   (fear)
2. "My son, if _____ entice you, do not consent." (1:10)
   (sinners)
3. "Happy is the man who finds _____ ." (3:13)
   (wisdom)
4. "My son, keep your father's commandment, and forsake not your _____ teaching." (6:20)
   (mother's)
5. "A _____ son makes a glad father." (10:1)
   (wise)
6. "A good man obtains favor from the _____ ." (12:2)
   (Lord)
7. "A soft answer turns away wrath, but a harsh word stirs up _____ ." (15:1)
   (anger)
8. "A man's mind plans his way, but the _____ directs his steps." (16:9)
   (Lord)
9. "Pride goes before _____ ." (16:18)
   (destruction)
10. "Trust in the Lord with all your _____ , and do not rely on your own insight." (3:5)
    (heart)

85. What Day of Creation?

Objective: To have a clear understanding of what God created on each day of creation week.

Materials Needed: None.

The Activity: Tell the children you will name certain items in nature. They are to tell on what day of creation God made it. If you have not studied the creation account recently, you should first review with the children the days of creation. Instead of reviewing the account in class you may wish to assign Genesis 1 for reading at home, and then do this activity. *Examples:*

Creation Days

First	*Second*	*Third*	*Fourth*	*Fifth*	*Sixth*
day	firmament	lilies	sun	doves	rabbit
night	separation	potatoes	moon	trout	Adam
light	of waters	dry land	stars	ducks	dinosaurs

86. Bible Word Spelling

Objective: To learn the correct spelling of well-chosen Bible words.

Materials Needed: Chalkboard, 26 3″ x 5″ cards.

The Activity: Prepare the 3″ x 5″ cards ahead of class time by writing the 26 letters of the alphabet on them. Depending on the size of your class, give two or three to each child until all are used. You will then pronounce a Bible word. The students having those letters will say and hold up their cards in the correct order to spell the word correctly. *Examples:* FAITH Students having those cards will say their letter(s) and hold it up in the correct order while you write each letter on the board. Use words such as: GOD, JESUS, PRAISE, BLESSED, MERCY, COMMAND-MENTS, RIGHTEOUSNESS, SALVATION. For some real fun try METHUSELAH, and MEPHIBOSHETH.

87. Prayer Chain

Objective: To share prayers within your group and jointly bring them to the heavenly Father.

Materials Needed: Construction paper, magic markers, glue or stapler.

The Activity: Cut strips from various colors of construction paper and give each child one of the strips. Ask the children to take a magic marker and write their prayer request, or prayer of thanks to God on the strip. Now tell them to illustrate or decorate their strip with the magic marker. When finished have a prayer time in which all may share their prayers within the group. When you are finished, ask them to glue or staple all strips together, end to end, into a "prayer chain." Display the chain in your room, and be sure to repeat this activity again when you feel the need. *Examples:*

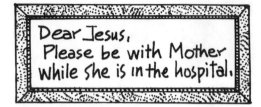

Dear Jesus,
Please be with Mother
while she is in the hospital.

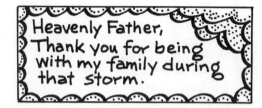

Heavenly Father,
Thank you for being
with my family during
that storm.

88. Symbols Fun

Objective: To become more proficient in identifying certain religious symbols.

Materials Needed: Paper, magic marker, slips of paper.

The Activity: Prepare simple sketches of religious symbols on flash cards or plain paper. As you hold up each card, the children are to write the name of the symbol on slips of paper you have given them. The child who recognizes all symbols is declared the winner. You may look in symbols books for ideas. *Examples:*

89. Let's Imagine

Objective: To experience the feeling of what took place in certain Bible narratives.

Materials Needed: Paper and pencils.

The Activity: Say to the children, "Let's imagine that you are one of the people in the crowd who saw and heard Jesus. You may close your eyes and when you open your eyes, write your feelings of what happened. What did you see, hear, smell, or touch? Close your eyes and imagine what took place when I give you the name of the Bible story. Ready?" *Examples:*

The Sermon on the Mount	Jesus Walking on the Water
Jesus Stilling the Tempest	Easter Morning at the Tomb
Jesus Feeding the 5,000	Triumphal Entry into Jerusalem

Allow sufficient time to think about the event. You may want to have soft music in the background for this activity. Give a tract to those who share their feelings with the group.

90. When Would You Sing These Hymns?

Objective: To become better acquainted with hymns used in various seasons of the church year.

Materials Needed: Your hymnbook.

The Activity: Prepare a list of well-known hymns from your hymnbook. Hymns should be chosen from these sections: Advent, Christmas, Epiphany, Lent, Easter, Morning, and Evening. Give the title of a hymn to the children, and ask them to tell when we would probably sing it. You may want to add other categories according to your needs: *Examples:*

1. Come, Thou Precious Ransom, Come (Advent)
2. Come to Calvary's Holy Mountain (Lent)
3. Abide with Me (Evening)
4. Oh, Come, All Ye Faithful (Christmas)
5. Jesus Christ Is Risen Today (Easter)
6. The Star Proclaims the King Is Here (Epiphany)
7. With the Lord Begin Thy Task (Morning)

91. Name That Tune

Objective: To give practice in recognizing hymns and songs.

Materials Needed: Cassette and player if necessary.

The Activity: If you are not musically inclined, ask your organist to record on a cassette some well-known hymns and songs of praise. Play the tunes, and ask the children to identify the hymn tune being played. Make sure you have a list of the tunes recorded in correct order. If you are musically inclined, you can hum the tune or play part of it on the piano. *Examples:* You may want to include: Beautiful Savior, I Know that My Redeemer Lives, Crown Him with Many Crowns, Take My Life and Let It Be, How Sweet the Name of Jesus Sounds, Rock of Ages, and Glory Be to Jesus.

92. Learning About Worship Services

Objective: To become familiar with parts of a worship service.

Materials Needed: None

The Activity: Write the following list of worship service parts on the chalkboard: Prelude, Postlude, Hymns, Confession of Sins, Scripture Readings, Psalms, Prayers, Lord's Prayer, Benediction, Lord's Supper, Baptism, Offering. Explain to the children that you will read a statement about one of these, and they are to tell which part of the service is being described. *Examples:*

1. What a Friend We Have in Jesus (Hymn)
2. "The Lord bless you and . . ." (Benediction)
3. "Thy kingdom come . . ." (Lord's Prayer)
4. "Take eat, this is . . ." (Lord's Supper)
5. "Again Jesus spoke to them saying . . ." (Scripture Reading)
6. "I baptize you in the . . ." (Holy Baptism)
7. Organist plays a musical selection at the beginning of the service. (Prelude)
8. Worshipers give money to the Lord. (Offering)

93. Favorite Hymns and Songs

Objective: To give practice in recognizing common hymns and Gospel songs.

Materials Needed: Your hymnal.

The Activity: Prepare a list of common hymns with which you feel the children should be acquainted. Give the title of a hymn to the class and leave out one of the words. Children are to give the missing word. *Examples:*

1. What a Friend We Have in _____ (Jesus)
2. Beautiful _____ (Savior)
3. Oh, Come, All Ye _____ (Faithful)
4. Abide, O _____ Jesus (Dearest)
5. In the Cross of _____ I Glory (Christ)
6. They'll Know We Are _____ by Our Love (Christians)
7. I Am _____ Thee, Lord Jesus (Trusting)

94. Feelings and Emotions

Objective: To recall Bible stories and tell what emotions they display.

Materials Needed: Chalkboard.

The Activity: Prepare a list of Bible stories which display the emotions or feelings mentioned below. Give the name of a Bible narrative and ask the children to tell what emotion or feeling it shows. You may wish to change your list of feelings from what is listed here. Limit the feelings to three for each game. *Examples:*

Game 1 Place on the chalkboard—FEAR, JOY, CALMNESS.

"What feeling does the Bible story show?"

The Destruction of Sodom and Gomorrah (fear)
The Blind Man Receives His Sight (joy)
The Prodigal Son Returns (joy)
The First Christmas Eve (calmness)
Jesus Stilling the Storm (fear and calmness)
Persecution of David by Saul (fear)

Game 2 Place on the chalkboard AMAZEMENT, SADNESS, SATISFACTION.

"What feeling do these Bible stories show?"

> The Feeding of the 5,000 (satisfaction)
> Creation Account (amazement)
> Jesus Dies on the Cross (sadness)
> The Draught of Fishes (satisfaction)
> Bringing Lazarus Back to Life (amazement)
> The Ten Lepers Healed (satisfaction or amazement)
> Jesus in Gethsemane (sadness)

95. What Would You Do?

Objective: To give practice in making correct choices.

Materials Needed: 3″ x 5″ cards.

The Activity: Prepare situation cards so that each child may draw one out of the box. They are to tell what the situation is and what they would do as a Christian boy or girl. *Examples:*

Bill's father asks him to cut the grass. Along comes Joe and asks him to play ball. What would you do?	Mary and Sue are friends. At school Mary hears some girls talking badly about Sue. What would you do?
Kathy heard from a classmate that her friend Cindy was telling others that she cheated in math. What would you do?	Jack and Tom are playing catch. Along comes a new boy and wants to play along. What would you do?

96. An Example to Follow?

Objective: To give practice in discerning which Bible people are good examples to follow.

Materials Needed: None.

The Activity: Prepare a list of Bible people and ask your class members to tell if the Bible person named would generally be a good example to follow or not. Children may answer with yes or no. *Examples:*

Absalom (No)	Solomon (No)	Mary (Yes)
Joseph (Yes)	Paul (Yes)	Stephen (Yes)
Jesus (Yes)	Ruth (Yes)	Queen Jezebel (No)
Abraham (Yes)	Jonah (No)	Jonathan (Yes)

97. Slide Presentation

Objective: To help children remember in sequence events of Bible narratives.

Materials Needed: Write-on slides, pencil colors, cassette recorder.

The Activity: Purchase a box of write-on slides from your local camera store. As a class project plan a slide presentation of a Bible narrative. Decide which scenes will be visualized, and what narration will be used. Appoint some children to work on the narration; and others to do the artwork. We have found that pencil colors work well on write-on slides. *Examples:* You may want to include the following in your selection of a Bible narrative:

1. Joseph Forgives His Brothers—Genesis 43—45
2. The Good Samaritan—Luke 10:25-37
3. The Great Catch of Fishes—Luke 5:1-11

98. A Bible Verse Search

Objective: To give practice in researching Bible verses and looking for a specific message.

Materials Needed: Chalkboard, Bibles, slips of paper, concordance.

The Activity: Prepare a list of Bible references on several chosen topics by looking in a concordance. Find enough references on the topic and write them on slips of paper. Each child will need to have a reference to look up. Place the references in a small box, and ask each child to take one. Tell them they are to look up the Bible verse on their slip of paper, and be ready to tell what their verse says about the topic. *Examples:*

Faith	*Creation*	*Forgive*
Matthew 17:20	Genesis 1:1	Psalm 86:5
Romans 10:17	Psalm 148:5	Jeremiah 31:34
Galatians 5:6	Isaiah 40:26	Matthew 6:12
Galatians 5:22	Isaiah 45:8	Matthew 6:14
Luke 17:5	Malachi 2:10	Matthew 9:6
Hebrews 11:1	Ephesians 3:9	Matthew 18:21
Habakkuk 2:4	Colossians 1:16	Mark 2:7
1 Corinthians 16:13	Revelation 10:6	Mark 11:25
2 Corinthians 13:5	Revelation 4:11	Luke 6:37
Titus 1:13	Romans 8:22	Luke 23:34

99. Getting to Know Each Other

Objective: To help each know the class members and teacher better.

Materials Needed: Bulletin board, individual pictures (snapshots), pencils, construction paper 9″ x 12″, rubber cement.

The Activity: Ask the children a week or two in advance to bring a favorite snapshot of themselves to class. Give each student a half sheet of construction paper, and tell them to paste the picture on the top of the page. After doing this, ask them to write a few sentences about themselves, school, home, likes, and dislikes. Place all of the finished displays on the bulletin board. The teacher should also do this.

100. Forget Me Not

Objective: To help children remember their experiences in church school.

Materials Needed: Poster board, paper, pencils, magic markers.

The Activity: In your last classes with your group ask the children to think about how others should remember them. This will then be placed on a Forget-Me-Not poster. The student may write a statement, or draw a sketch, and sign his name to it. They may choose likes or dislikes, some event, or a statement about the class. When completed, all items are placed on the Forget-Me-Not poster. *Example:* "I am the girl who asked so many questions."—Susan Jones "I like Sunday School."—Mark Smith

Usage Chart

Indicate date and grade used

1. Location of Bible Cities   _____

2. What Is It?   _____

3. What Picture Would You Take?   _____

4. Who Made the Headlines?   _____

5. Jordan, Red Sea, or Sea of Galilee   _____

6. Inalnd or Ports   _____

7. I Visited . . .   _____

8. I Wish to Know   _____

9. Where Did They Meet?   _____

10. Another Name   _____

11. What's Wrong with the Location?   _____

12. Going to Bible Places   _____

13. Bible Geography   _____

14. How Far Is It?   _____

15. Bible Quiz—Game 1   _____

16. Bible Quiz—Game 2   _____

17. Choose a Bible Friend   _____

18. Put On Your Thinking Caps   _____

19. Miracles and Parables   _____

20. What Was Their Work?   _____

21. Who Said It?   _____

22. The Bible Says So, I Believe It   _____

23. Question Box   _____

24. Prophet, Priest, or King   _____

25. Remember Me? _____

26. Who and What _____

27. Bible Synonyms _____

28. Furniture in Bible Homes _____

29. Chalkboard Fun _____

30. Bible Nouns _____

31. Foods of Bible Times _____

32. Plants of the Bible _____

33. Plants and Animals Bible Stories _____

34. Bible Animals _____

35. Name the Bible Bird _____

36. Weather Phenomena _____

37. Finish the Bible Verse _____

38. Bible Money _____

39 Person, Place, or Object _____

40. Kings, Women, or Prophets _____

41. Whose Father or Mother _____

42. Who's the Main Character? _____

43. My Favorite Bible City _____

44. Whose City? _____

45. What's the Message? _____

46. I Spent the Day With . . . _____

47. Old or New Testament Events _____

48. Old or New Testament Places _____

49. Identify the Bible Book—Old Testament _____

50. Identify the Bible Book—New Testament _____

51. How Did They Do It? _____

52. How Was Life Different? _____

53. Bible Words Review _____

54. Bible Alphabet _____

55. Christmas, Lent, Easter _____

56. Numbers from the Bible _____

57. Hunting for Bible Treasures _____

58. Who Am I? _____

59. Bible Word Building _____

60. A Forbidden Word _____

61. Jumbled Bible Words _____

62. Scrambled Bible Verses _____

63. Bible Pen Pals _____

64. Finish the Bible Story _____

65. Spelling Bible Words _____

66. Bible Chronology _____

67. Beat the Clock _____

68. Know Your Bible Chapters _____

69. Know the Psalms _____

70. In Which Book of the Bible? _____

71. Guess Who _____

72. Bible Story Question Cards _____

73. The Ten Commandments _____

74. Which Commandment? _____

75. Finish the Commandment _____

76. Find the Object _____

77. Name the Roman _____

78. Bible Pictures _____

79. Bible Word Association _____

80. Find the Key Word _____

81. Flannelboard Fun _____

82. Objects and People Association _____

83. Three Questions _____

84. Wisdom from Proverbs _____

85. What Day of Creation? _____

86. Bible Word Spelling _____

87. Prayer Chain _____

88. Symbols Fun _____

89. Let's Imagine _____

90. When Would You Sing These Hymns? _____

91. Name That Tune _____

92. Learning About Worship Services _____

93. Favorite Hymns and Songs _____

94. Feelings and Emotions _____

95. What Would You Do? _____

96. An Example to Follow? _____

97. Slide Presentation _____

98. A Bible Verse Search _____

99. Getting to Know Each Other _____

100. Forget Me Not _____

Notes

Notes

Notes

Notes

Notes

Notes